YOUR FIRST THIRTY DAYS

Building a Professional Image in a New Job

Elwood N. Chapman

CRISP PUBLICATIONS, INC.
Los Altos, California

YOUR FIRST THIRTY DAYS
Building a Professional Image in a New Job

Elwood N. Chapman

CREDITS
Editor: **Michael G. Crisp and Tony Hicks**
Designer: **Carol Harris**
Typesetting: **Interface Studio**
Cover Design: **Carol Harris**
Artwork: **Ralph Mapson**

Copyright © 1990 by Crisp Publications, Inc.
Printed in the United States of America

Crisp books are distributed in Canada by Reid Publishing, Ltd., P.O. Box 7267, Oakville, Ontario, Canada L6J 6L6.

In Australia by Career Builders, P.O. Box 1051, Springwood, Brisbane, Queensland, Australia 4127.

And in New Zealand by Career Builders, P.O. Box 571, Manurewa, New Zealand.

Library of Congress Catalog Card Number 89-81250
Chapman, Elwood N.
Your First Thirty Days
ISBN 1-56052-003-5

ABOUT THIS BOOK

YOUR FIRST THIRTY DAYS is not like most books. It stands out from other self-help books in an important way. It's not a book to read—it's a book to *use*. The unique week-by-week self-paced format and the many worksheets encourage the reader to apply what is learned on a day-by-day basis in making her or his successful transition into a new work environment.

The objective of YOUR FIRST THIRTY DAYS is to help new employees make a successful adjustment to their new job. Using this book is a WIN-WIN situation—employees will get off to a faster start and enhance their careers. Management will benefit from higher productivity, sooner.

YOUR FIRST THIRTY DAYS (and other titles listed in the back of this book) can be used effectively in a number of ways. Here are some possibilities:

—**Individual Study.** Because the book is self-instructional, all that is needed is a quiet place, some time and a pencil. With YOUR FIRST THIRTY DAYS it is recommended that the reader go over the entire book before reporting to work and then refer to it page by page on a week-to-week basis. Used in this manner, the book will take the reader through the first thirty days with fewer problems and greater success.

—**Orientation Programs and Seminars.** After basic company rules, medical benefits, retirement plans, etc., are taken care of, YOUR FIRST THIRTY DAYS can be passed out to new employees to complete their orientation. If only one or two hours are available, early pages can be discussed and the employee can complete the book on a day-by-day basis in a contract with his or her supervisor. (See page 3.)

—**Remote Location Training.** Books can be sent to those not able to attend "home office" training sessions.

There are several other possibilities that depend on the objectives, orientation program or ideas of the user.

One thing for sure: even after it has been read, this book will be looked at—and thought about—again and again.

The true meaning of being a professional is living up to the many standards of your career area (ethical and otherwise) regardless of where and for whom you work.

WHY THIRTY DAYS?

There are many reasons why a practical, thirty-day improvement program makes sense to ambitious career people. A few are listed below:

- Thirty days is long enough to demonstrate to yourself and your peers that measurable progress is happening on the job. It gives you enough time to demonstrate your potential to others.

- Thirty days is not so long that you or others will become discouraged by your progress and give up. You can keep a clear focus on your goals and reward yourself for reaching them.

- Behavioral changes are usually achieved only after a strong commitment is made. People are more apt to commit themselves deeply for thirty days than for a longer period. For example, dropouts are not unusual in 18-week college courses, but more rare in shorter courses.

- Another major advantage is that a thirty-day period divides nicely into four weeks. Most career people do their work and lifestyle planning on a week-to-week basis. This book is organized to take advantage of that excellent habit. After each week you will review your progress and set new goals for the next week.

The thirty-day system works. Give it a try!

TO THE EMPLOYER

Your First Thirty Days was designed as a supplement and extension to any new-employee orientation program. This book can help a beginning employee make a more successful and complete adjustment. When this happens, there are several benefits to management including:

- Higher productivity levels.

- Improved human relations. New employees will integrate themselves more smoothly into their respective "teams."

- Reduced employee turnover. Nothing will keep a new employee with an organization longer than the pride that comes from being accepted, making a contribution, and receiving recognition for it.

For best results, *Your First Thirty Days* should be provided to new employees at the end of their orientation program. They should also be encouraged to initiate a contract with their immediate supervisor. This contract is simply an agreement to have both the new employee and the supervisor complete the evaluation on page 61 at the end of the employee's first thirty days. For accountability purposes, both assessments could be returned to the Training Director or other individual for review.

In those cases where a formal orientation program is not available or company literature in this area is limited, *Your First Thirty Days* is recommended as an excellent substitute for an in-house program.

TO THE NEW EMPLOYEE

Thirty days from now, you will have become a professional member of the organization you have joined (or missed out on an excellent opportunity). This book is designed to help you enjoy progress in your new job without making unnecessary mistakes, so you can feel good about yourself.

The person who gave you *Your First Thirty Days* has confidence you will make the best possible use of it. This means you should follow it page by page, week by week. Then at the end of thirty days you should meet with your supervisor to evaluate your progress. You may wish to read the book right through and then reread it page by page as you advance through your first thirty days on your new job. It is suggested that you assess your progress at the end of each week. Forms are provided to help you do this. It will then be possible for you to set goals for the following week.

A successful adjustment to your new job will give you greater confidence in yourself. Your new co-workers and superiors will also notice your progress, and when this happens, you will gain acceptance and recognition. You will know you have launched your career successfully.

Good luck!

Elwood N. Chapman

Elwood N. Chapman

CONTENTS

CONTENTS (Continued)

PREPARATION

GETTING READY FOR YOUR
FIRST DAY ON THE JOB

I'm a great believer in luck, and I find
the harder I work the more of it I have.
—Thomas Jefferson

THE CHALLENGE!

When you join a new organization (or move into a new assignment) you become the "new kid on the block." This means that all eyes will be upon you until you are accepted as a member of your new team. During this period regular employees (including superiors) will observe your behavior. They will be looking for answers to the following questions:

- How long will it take you to carry a full share of the work load? Are your skills up to par? Will you pitch in and help others? Will you be on the job every day?

- Will you be human-relations "smart"? That is, will you be sensitive to the needs of those ahead of you? Will you side with co-workers who are negative, or will you play it cool and treat everyone the same way?

- How successful will you be at winning over those co-workers and superiors who are critical? Will you know how to handle their testing? Will you be able to stand your ground and win the respect of co-workers and superiors alike?

In thirty days, these questions and many others will have been answered. If you are successful, you will have demonstrated that you are a professional, and your co-workers will support and encourage your future progress.

You will have met the challenge!

VOLUNTARY
CONTRACT*

(You are encouraged to have this informal contract signed by your immediate supervisor your first day on the job.)

AS A NEW EMPLOYEE, I AGREE TO MAKE THE BEST POSSIBLE USE OF THIS BOOK TO HELP ME ADJUST TO MY NEW ASSIGNMENT. WHEN MY FIRST MONTH IS OVER, I AGREE TO COMPLETE THE EVALUATION OF THIRTY-DAY WORK PERFORMANCE FORM ON PAGE 61 AND TO PROVIDE A COPY FOR MY SUPERVISOR TO COMPLETE AND DISCUSS.

At the end of thirty days, I will meet with my supervisor to review my progress and establish action steps for even greater progress in the future.

_____

Signature of Employee

_____

Signature of Supervisor

_____

Date of thirty-day evaluation meeting

*This agreement can be initiated by a new employee, by his or her supervisor, or by the person in charge of orientation. The purpose is to provide a degree of accountability to help a new employee adjust to the future.

BE A COMFORTABLE PERSON TO MEET

As a stranger to your new co-workers, it is only natural that you will be studied and reacted to. You will attract attention because you constitute a change in the work environment. Whether you transmit a favorable image or not depends primarily upon your friendliness and grooming.

To communicate friendliness, you need to be a comfortable person to meet. This means you avoid behaviors that might communicate you feel ''above'' or ''beneath'' those you are joining. It is important to relax, smile, and become a team member without creating unnecessary waves.

It is also important to communicate a positive visual image by paying attention to your appearance (without overdoing it).

To help you prepare, some specific grooming areas are presented below. Combined they constitute the physical image you will communicate. Rate yourself in each area by circling the appropriate number. A 5 indicates no further improvement is possible. A 3 or lower indicates improvement is needed.

	High				Low
1. Hairstyle, hair grooming (neat/clean)	5	4	3	2	1
2. Personal hygiene (clean fingernails, etc.)	5	4	3	2	1
3. Appearance of clothing (clean, pressed)	5	4	3	2	1
4. Appropriate shoes (clean, polished)	5	4	3	2	1
5. Choice of clothing (not too casual)	5	4	3	2	1
6. Choice of clothing (appropriate for the work environment)	5	4	3	2	1
7. Accessories (not too wild)	5	4	3	2	1
8. Once you are ready, look in the mirror. Is this just how you want to look your first day on the job?	5	4	3	2	1

Naturally, your attitude toward meeting new co-workers is the key. The moment they sense you have a sincere desire to join their group (and you are willing to make their jobs easier through your contributions) you will be on your way toward full acceptance.

GETTING READY CHECKLIST

Before reporting for work, you will feel more confident and professional if you do the following:

☐ Have a pocket notebook where you can write down special instructions, directions, and names you need to remember.

☐ Make certain you have transportation. Have you had your car checked recently? Do you know the correct bus schedule?

☐ Decide on the best route in order to avoid traffic problems and frustrations. Have you made parking arrangements ahead of time?

☐ If you have a small child, work out the details of your child care arrangements. Do you have a backup solution? Will your arrangements allow you to give full concentration to your job?

☐ If you have older children, will they be fully instructed on how to take care of themselves without calling you on the job except in emergencies?

☐ Cut back on outside commitments during your first thirty days. Would a weekend ski or cycling trip drain you for Monday morning? Many new employees overextend themselves and miss a day of work when it counts the most.

☐ Work out your wardrobe for the first week to present your best image.*

☐ Have a regular exercise schedule in place.

☐ Take care of needed dental, medical, or other professional appointments ahead of time.

Through advanced planning, professional people avoid asking for time away from their jobs. *Especially during the first thirty days of a new job.*

---

*For excellent books on looking professional, consider ordering *Always in Style* if you are a woman, or *Successful Style* if you are a man. Write to Crisp Publications, Inc., 95 First Street, Los Altos, CA 94022.

WHAT TO EXPECT

It's happened! You are moving into a new position that shows promise. What can you anticipate? On the left is the good news. On the right are some challenges you may face before the first week is over.

GOOD NEWS

Your employer has confidence in you or you would not have been selected in the first place.

Your ability to contribute will be respected by your co-workers.

Your organization wants you to experience personal growth.

You are a valuable asset and the more you learn the more valuable you will be.

You obviously have confidence in yourself or you wouldn't have accepted the position.

You will not be expected to work with maximum efficiency in the beginning.

You probably were hired as much for what you can learn as for what you already know.

CHALLENGES

You may be working for a demanding supervisor.

You may not receive all of the help you would like or need.

Not everyone will welcome you with open arms.

Your new working environment (including the negative attitudes of fellow-workers) may not be everything you had hoped for.

You may find you need to upgrade your skills in a hurry.

There may be some pressures you did not anticipate.

You may discover you are more fatigued at the end of the day than you expected.

There is no such thing as a *perfect* supervisor, working environment, or organization. Your challenge is to make the most out of what you find on a day-to-day basis and move ahead. In thirty days, after you have had the opportunity to see the big picture, you can make a more perceptive and accurate evaluation.

LEARNING THE ROPES

Every organization has its own special culture. This means that individuals who make up your new environment have their own customs, habits, and performance standards. To be fully accepted into their world, you will have to honor their ways of operating and adjust accordingly. You must become a part of the team in order to make a full contribution to productivity. If you isolate yourself, your contribution will be less than it should be.

How do you learn the ropes in your new environment? Here are three suggestions:

- Read all of the company literature available. Study personnel procedures. Learn about benefits to avoid asking unnecessary questions. Until you learn the rules, you cannot be a professional player.

- Learn the unwritten rules of the game. Talk to people. Be observant. What behavior is tolerated but frowned upon? What behavior would be approved by your supervisor but turn co-workers against you—and vice versa?

- Try to find out how new employees have excelled or gotten into trouble in the past. Ask your supervisor for feedback. Ask professional co-workers for suggestions. The idea here is to avoid typical traps that could cause your fellow employees to reject you as a professional.

If you are fortunate enough to have gone through a well-designed orientation program before reading this book, you have a big advantage. Rethink what you learned during orientation and then use *Your First Thirty Days* to put it to work. If you did not have a formal orientation, use this book as a guide to becoming a professional. Simply take things page by page and week by week until you are over the hump.

BE A TEAM PLAYER

When you start a new job nothing is more important to your future than becoming a good team player. What does this mean?

It has to do with *timing*. That is, being at the right place at the right time so you can make your best contribution to the total operation of the department or team. It is a little like scoring a run in baseball.

Being at your work
station when needed

Getting things
done on time

Getting to work
on time

Putting it all
together

FIRST BASE: You get to first base when you arrive at work on time in good physical shape with an attitude that says "I am ready to contribute." *OTHER TEAM MEMBERS DON'T HAVE TO WAIT AROUND GETTING UPSET WHILE YOU STRUGGLE TO GET STARTED.*

SECOND BASE: You arrive at second base when you return from your breaks and lunch on time so you don't upset the flow of work. *OTHER TEAM MEMBERS ARE NOT FORCED TO ANSWER YOUR TELEPHONE CALLS OR TO ANSWER QUESTIONS REGARDING YOUR ABSENCE.*

THIRD BASE: You put yourself in scoring position when you get your assigned tasks accomplished on time. *OTHER TEAM MEMBERS ARE NOT HELD UP BECAUSE YOUR PART OF THE JOB IS BEING NEGLECTED.* (For example, a bus boy in a restaurant who is slow cleaning up and setting a table is not only causing customers to wait but is also slowing down the entire team operation.)

HOME BASE: Getting home (scoring) is being a team member others can depend upon. When you function in concert with co-workers (doing your part at the right time), *EVERYBODY WINS.*

Doing a quality job is important. Doing it at the right time is also important. The new employee who can accomplish both within a few days is the one who finds immediate acceptance among co-workers and superiors.

UNDERSTANDING PRODUCTIVITY

Regardless of the organization (or new department) you join, your ultimate future will depend on your personal productivity. For the purpose of this book, productivity means the total contribution you finally make to your firm. And make no mistake—productivity is always measured!

It is relatively easy to measure the productivity of some employees, such as a salesperson, because results (sales) show up with numbers. On the other hand, the productivity of other employees, such as a flight attendant, is more difficult to measure. Intangibles such as providing routine service to passengers and handling difficult situations do not show up in any figures. But even when everyone's productivity is measured, intangibles are involved.

Different organizations assess productivity in different ways. They may focus on:

- Minimum acceptable performance—which may not always be clearly defined or communicated.
- Average performance—the mean of all employee productivity on identical jobs.
- Excellence—i.e., the degree of excellence that each new employee is expected to reach in time.

Please study the illustration below.

PRODUCTIVITY SCALE

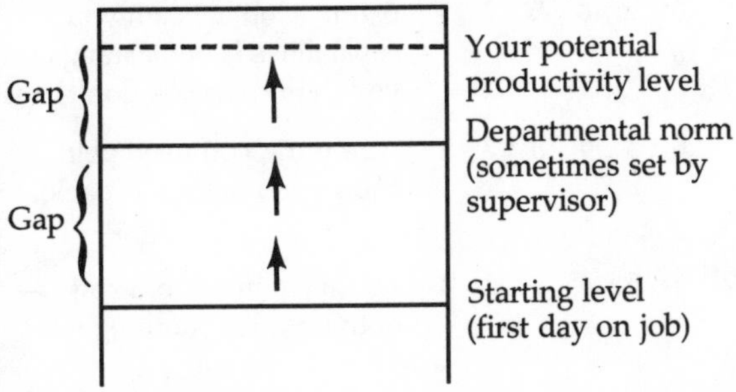
Gap
Gap
Your potential productivity level
Departmental norm (sometimes set by supervisor)
Starting level (first day on job)

You will notice there is a large gap between the starting level of the new employee and the departmental norm—the average productivity of employees in similar jobs. Your challenge is to move your productivity up to the norm as quickly as possible. Depending upon the job itself, this may take more or less than thirty days.

There is a smaller gap between the expected norm and your potential productivity level. Once you match the performance of other employees, you should strive to get closer to your potential. Although there will always be a gap between what you could do and what you actually accomplish, the smaller the gap the better.

LEARNING ATTITUDE SCALE

More than any other factor, your personal attitude toward learning will be the key to your success during your first thirty days on the job. To help you become aware of this (and also become more confident and positive), please complete the following scale. Circle the 10 if you agree 100 percent with the statement. Circle the 1 if you are in total disagreement. Most people fall somewhere in the middle.

It is best to start a job knowing you have plenty to learn.	10 9 8 7 6 5 4 3 2 1	It is best to rely on the knowledge you already have.
Do it their way until you *know* you have a better way.	10 9 8 7 6 5 4 3 2 1	Do it your own way until you're told to do it differently.
There is usually more than one way to do a job right.	10 9 8 7 6 5 4 3 2 1	There is usually only one way to do a job right.
Humility in a star performer is as important as in a rookie.	10 9 8 7 6 5 4 3 2 1	Humility in a star performer is unnecessary and ridiculous.
Learning during your first thirty days can be more important than productivity.	10 9 8 7 6 5 4 3 2 1	Management doesn't care about learning, only about productivity.
Asking questions communicates a good learning attitude.	10 9 8 7 6 5 4 3 2 1	Asking questions irritates co-workers and makes you look stupid.
It shows a good attitude to say you want to learn.	10 9 8 7 6 5 4 3 2 1	Saying you want to learn demonstrates insecurity on your part.
Doing a job beneath your capabilities with a smile on your face shows you can take it.	10 9 8 7 6 5 4 3 2 1	Doing a job beneath your capabilities is demeaning and you should say you don't like it.
Admitting you need help is better than making mistakes.	10 9 8 7 6 5 4 3 2 1	Admitting you need help shows you are not capable.
You were hired more for what you can learn than for what you already know.	10 9 8 7 6 5 4 3 2 1	You were hired to do a job—nothing more, nothing less.

TOTAL [   ]

A score of 70 or more indicates you know the importance of a learning attitude no matter how much experience or education you may have. A score of under 70 indicates you might get off to a better start if you use your first thirty days learning more and demonstrating less.

THE FIRST DAY

Can you remember the events that took place your first day on your last job? Some people, even after thirty years have elapsed, remember many details. Why is this?

The primary reason is because so much is at stake. You want to prove to yourself and others that you can handle things. You want to make the most out of your new career opportunity. And you want to be accepted by your co-workers. No wonder most new employees are nervous.

The loyalty you may or may not feel after your first day is very important. If you are ignored, shuffled around, or embarrassed, you may hold a resentment that can last for years. It may cause your attitude to be less positive. But if people go out of their way to be friendly and some immediate bonding takes place, you are apt to become loyal and productive immediately. If your attitude starts out positive, it will probably continue that way.

The point is that your first day is so critical to your future that you can't afford to take chances. The following suggestions are made:

- Admit you are nervous, but demonstrate a sincere willingness to learn and adjust.

- Don't wait for others to be nice to you. Extend your own hand of friendship from the very beginning.

- Communicate an open, positive attitude through a smile and other gestures. When appropriate, enjoy a good laugh.

In other words, *make* your first day a success regardless of the difficulties you may face.

WARDROBE AND GROOMING ADJUSTMENTS

On page 4 a few grooming suggestions were made to help you communicate your best image the first day on your new job. After getting the lay of the land as far as dress standards are concerned, most people make adjustments. Check the following examples.

☐ Estelle was more enthusiastic about her new office job than she expected, but she was not prepared for the sophistication and high-fashion image her co-workers communicated. Result? Estelle shifted toward the top end of her wardrobe, took more care in coordinating, and devoted more time to selecting jewelry and making up her face. It didn't affect her productivity, but it made her more comfortable.

☐ In an attempt to make a good impression his first day on the job, Greg dressed like he was going to a wedding. He soon discovered that his department (drafting) was rather casual. Two employees wore jeans. Result? Greg took off his coat and tie and the following day (careful not to go overboard) wore slacks, a conservative sport shirt, and loafers.

☐ Jerri accepted her new job knowing she would have to wear a prescribed uniform. The prospect didn't thrill her. Within a few days (after receiving more than one compliment) she discovered the standard uniform allowed her to highlight her facial makeup and her hair. Result? She relaxed and decided to take advantage of the situation.

☐ Jake, accepting his first job in a department store, was amazed at the high dress standards. In discussing the matter with his supervisor over a soft drink, his superior said: "It is not only what you wear but how you keep your hair and beard trimmed, cleanliness, and all that goes with it that is important here. Our customers are sophisticated and our management is demanding. Hope you can adjust."

☐ The first hour on her new job Maria knew she was overdressed. Result? She carried it off well the first day and then slowly moved into attire that was less trendy and more suited to business.

New employees should not feel pressured into buying expensive new clothes in order to feel comfortable in their work environments. In almost all cases, taking a new look at an old wardrobe, careful coordinating, and special attention to hair and facial grooming will do the trick.

SUGGESTION

Your general preparation is complete. You are now ready to start your first week on the new job.

After your second day, read the next 12 pages under one of the following plans:

- Read and study all the WEEK ONE pages at once.

- Read and study two pages each night after work.

- Read all the WEEK ONE pages ahead of time and then review them one by one during the week.

Whatever the procedure you work out the first week, follow it for the next three weeks.

Doing this will improve your progress and keep you from making unnecessary mistakes.

WELCOME!

WEEK ONE

GETTING THE LAY
OF THE LAND

Do what you can, with what you have,
where you are.
—Theodore Roosevelt

REMEMBERING NAMES

Unless you work for a very small organization, you will meet many people your first few days on the job. If you try to remember everyone's name at once, you may become confused and be embarrassed. The best bet may be to remember a few each day. Most people find it a big help to write the name of each person they meet in a pocket notebook. This will allow you to get the full name and the correct spelling. Most important, it allows you to refer to your notebook at night so you can recall the meeting, remember the face, and practice saying the name a few times.

Madelyn Burley-Allen in her book *Memory Skills in Business** presents the following steps to use in remembering names:

SEVEN STEPS TO SUCCESS

Following is a simple seven-step process to remember names:

1. Have a positive mental set.

2. Be interested in remembering each person's name.

3. Listen attentively to the name and, if unsure what it is, ask for a spelling.

4. Form an association to something you are familiar with (perhaps with someone else that has a similar name).

5. Use the substitution process by substituting the name with a silly picture, or with something you're familiar with, such as:

   Ruth—Baby Ruth candy bar

   Bill—Thousand dollar bill

6. Link the silly picture to the person's name.

7. Repeat the name and substitution (or association) until you are confident you know it.

Give yourself a full week to learn the names of key superiors and immediate co-workers. If you learn and remember ten names the first week, you are doing well. By the end of your first thirty days you should be able to expand your list to thirty or more names.

Memory Skills in Business may be ordered using the form in the back of this book.

YOU CAN'T LEARN UNLESS YOU LISTEN!*

Effective listening is the key to success in any working environment. Good listening is especially important the first few days on a new job. You will be receiving instructions on organizational policies and procedures, as well as job instructions (what to do, how to operate new equipment, what your specific responsibilities will be, etc.).

If you fail to listen on a new job, you may miss a safety instruction that could prevent an injury. If you fail to listen you may later make a mistake that causes a key customer to go to a competitor. You may accidentally damage a piece of expensive equipment. Or you may miss out on an important benefit (such as profit sharing) for yourself. It pays to listen!

How can you improve your listening skills for the critical days ahead? ANSWER THE STATEMENTS BELOW AND RATE YOURSELF.

	YES	NO
1. I will listen to what is being said rather than evaluate who is saying it.	☐	☐
2. I will listen with my eyes as well as my ears.	☐	☐
3. I will refrain from interrupting until I am sure I have received the message correctly.	☐	☐
4. If I am not sure about the message, I will repeat it to the giver and ask if I've got it right.	☐	☐
5. I will write down complicated or specially important messages for review later.	☐	☐
6. I will make sure I am in the best physical position to hear the message.	☐	☐
7. I will keep my nervousness under control	☐	☐
8. I will concentrate and not fake my attention.	☐	☐
9. I *want* to hear every message.	☐	☐
10. I will be a patient listener.	☐	☐

If you gave yourself 8 or more ''yes'' answers, you appear to be ready for your first few days in your new work environment. Keep in mind that your supervisor and co-workers will know whether or not you are a good listener before the first week is over.

---

*The Business of Listening by Diane Bone may be ordered using the form in the back of this book.

18

TELEPHONE TIPS

Chances are good your new job will involve some use of the telephone, perhaps extensive use. Either way, telephone courtesy is important to your firm and your success. Ten basic but vital tips are listed below. As you check them out, keep in mind that one way to improve your telephone courtesy at work is to start practicing some tips at home.

Check the items you need to work on:

☐ Hold the transmitter portion of the telephone directly in front of your mouth. If you hold it too far away from your mouth you risk not being understood.

☐ Avoid side conversations of any kind during a telephone conversation. The person on the phone deserves your full attention.

☐ Never eat or drink while talking. If your mouth is full when the telephone rings, wait a few seconds before answering.

☐ Answer in as few rings as possible. A maximum of three rings is a good standard.

☐ When you place a caller on hold to answer another line or take care of an emergency, ask for permission and wait for an answer.

☐ Put a smile into your voice. It's easy to do. Simply remember to smile as you answer a call. Believe it or not, your voice will sound friendlier.

☐ Whenever possible, use the caller's name. It is also courteous to use ''Sir'' or ''Ma'am'' in conversations.

☐ Use these four answering courtesies: Greet the caller. State your organization (or department). Introduce yourself by name. Offer your help.

☐ Do not rush the caller. Listen carefully before you give your answer.

☐ When you finish your telephone conversation be sure to do one or all of the following: Thank the person for calling. If it's a customer, let them know you appreciate their business. Give an assurance that any promise you've made will be fulfilled. Leave the other person with a positive feeling.

---

*For more information, read *Telephone Courtesy & Customer Service* by Lloyd C. Finch. Ordering information is at the back of this book.

HOW MUCH PRODUCTIVITY IN WEEK ONE?

How much you produce (and prepare yourself to produce) is the key to your early success on the job.

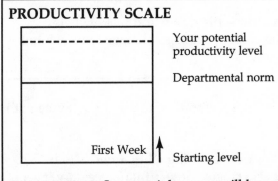

PRODUCTIVITY SCALE

Your potential productivity level

Departmental norm

First Week

Starting level

You will want to demonstrate measurable progress in productivity as soon as possible. In reaching for the departmental norm, however, do not neglect what you need to learn. And don't ignore your relationships with co-workers and superiors. It is the combination of productivity, learning, and work relationships that will provide long-term progress. In most jobs, you will be expected to produce less at the beginning, so you usually have time to improve in all directions.

So how fast should your productivity improve? Here are three strategies to consider:

Strategy #1: MODEST PRODUCTIVITY—MAXIMUM PROGRESS IN HUMAN RELATIONS. This means you operate slightly beneath your productivity capacity and concentrate on building good relationships with those around you.

Strategy #2: HIGH PRODUCTIVITY—MINIMUM ATTENTION TO HUMAN RELATIONS. Most of your energy goes into job tasks and only a small amount into building relationships. You do this because you feel others want you to carry your full load quickly, rather than make progress in other directions.

Strategy #3: GOOD PRODUCTIVITY—GOOD HUMAN RELATIONS PROGRESS. The idea here is to balance your progress in both directions—show above-average speed in reaching higher productivity and work on building human relations at the same time.

Your choice of stategies depends upon various factors. These could include:

Instructions from your supervisor. Your boss may say something like this: We are behind schedule, so I would appreciate your concentrating on getting work out. You'll have time to deal with other matters later.''

Attitude of Co-workers. Your fellow-employees may not give you the chance to build relationships with them until you demonstrate that you are a good worker and are willing to carry your load.

Customer Involvement. If you have customer contact the first day or so on your new job, *the customer comes first.* Everything else, including relationships with others who also have customer contact, takes second place.

QUALITY STARTS DAY ONE

Please study the statement below. It was made by a capable employee during her first week on a new job.

> "If I can get by the first month, then I can settle down and make whatever changes are necessary for outstanding career progress. Management will not expect perfection from me at the beginning."

What kind of work and learning attitude does she transmit? See if you agree with the reaction of the author.

1. A "get by" attitude might prevent her from learning all that needs to be learned for future progress. It could also create a lower than necessary level of performance, which could lose her the respect of other team members before she finally gets around to demonstrating her potential.

AGREE ☐   DISAGREE ☐

2. The intention to "settle down" after the first month might mean she starts off with poor work habits and sloppy performance. This could continue after the first days are over. Such an attitude violates the principle, "Do it right the first time."

AGREE ☐   DISAGREE ☐

3. The phrase "management will not expect perfection" denies that work environments have standards. Superiors expect new employees to reach standards step by step. Translated, this means they want to see progress toward reaching standards from day one.

AGREE ☐   DISAGREE ☐

In the author's view, striving for quality is always a winning strategy. The sooner it starts the better. The only way to reach acceptable standards at a later date is to practice quality from the start. The new employee should resist any pressure to get the job done at the sacrifice of quality.

Completing the exercise on the following page will reveal some additional aspects of "quality control."

QUALITY AWARENESS EXERCISE

Consider each statement and mark it true or false based on your current awareness of the quality aspects in your work and personal life. Answers and author's comments are listed at the bottom of the page.

TRUE	FALSE	
_____	_____	**1.** Quality means preventing problems rather than picking up the pieces afterward.
_____	_____	**2.** Quality is represented in the little things as well as the big ones.
_____	_____	**3.** Most new employees want to do quality work.
_____	_____	**4.** Personal quality standards and business quality standards have little in common.
_____	_____	**5.** Customers, co-workers, and superiors pay little attention to quality.
_____	_____	**6.** People who talk about quality are idealists, not realists.
_____	_____	**7.** Quality takes time to achieve.
_____	_____	**8.** Quality means conforming to a set of personal standards.
_____	_____	**9.** Company quality expectations are best communicated informally by word of mouth.
_____	_____	**10.** Quality requires commitment.

SCORE [　　]

ANSWERS: 1-3: True. 4: False (Employees with high personal standards are usually the ones who lead business quality programs). 5: False (Customers, and most supervisors and co-workers, are often picky about quality). 6: False (People who talk about quality are realists). 7-8: True. 9: False (It is best when quality guidelines come from the top, are in writing, and are agreed upon by employees). 10: True.

---

*The above exercise was modeled after one contained in the fifty-minute book *Quality at Work* by Diane Bone and Rick Griggs. For ordering information, see the back of this book.

PACING IS EVERYTHING*

Some new employees are so eager to succeed that they set an initial pace that is so fast it leads them into trouble. They are so intense about making a good showing that they make needless job-oriented mistakes, offend co-workers, or wind up with a ''flash in the pan'' or ''eager beaver'' image that they never live down.

Professionals set a slower, steady pace. They are not as concerned about where they are at the beginning as where they will be in thirty days. They know that it takes time to learn new tasks, build sound human relationships, and ultimately make a team contribution. They recognize that it is their responsibility to fit in to the existing environment first. Only then will they be in a position to offer suggestions for improvement and contribute on a high level.

This guide is designed to teach you the kind of pace that will minimize mistakes and enhance your professional image. For example, you will be encouraged to increase your personal productivity at a pace that will take you higher without sacrificing human relationships. To accomplish this goal, it is recommended that you check your progress on a week-to-week basis. Take your adventure one day at a time, but *consolidate* your gains each week and start over. To encourage this approach, each of your first four weeks has been assigned a goal or theme.

The ideal time to review your weekly progress, consolidate your gains, and prepare your goals for the following week is when you feel most comfortable. In doing this, you may wish to refer to your notebook, isolate any problems that have surfaced, and talk things over with someone seriously concerned with your professional future.

Personal Time Management by Marion E. Haynes is an excellent book on this subject. It may be ordered using the form in the back of this book.

CASE #1: RESCUE

Patti felt confident and pleased after the two-day orientation program for new employees. However, she was not prepared for the sophistication, skill level, and fast tempo found in the department to which she was assigned. By noon of her first real day of work, Patti viewed herself as underprepared, underskilled, and underdressed. Fortunately, on her way to the company cafeteria one of her new co-workers, Ethel, caught up with her and they had lunch together.

During lunch, Patti received many tips and suggestions. For example, she learned from Ethel that Mr. Gregg, their manager, was in trouble with his superiors. That Jill who has a work station next to Patti spreads rumors and is not to be trusted. That Mrs. K, the senior programmer, was recently divorced and is working overtime to escape from her personal life. Ethel was so friendly that Patti began to feel more confident. She was pleased when Ethel suggested they meet after work for a drink. Ethel's closing remarks were: "Once you get the lay of the land around here you will be able to protect yourself and survive."

What appears to be happening? What mistake may Patti be making? What advice would you give her?

_____

_____

_____

_____

_____

_____

_____

_____

_____

_____

See page 64 to compare your thoughts with those of the author.

YOU AND YOUR SUPERVISOR

Your most important working relationship is with your immediate supervisor. Three basic factors are involved in building and maintaining such a relationship: productivity, cooperation with co-workers, and communication with your boss.

Your supervisor is responsible for departmental productivity. As is true with individuals, there is always a gap between what is accomplished and what could be accomplished within a department. The sooner you close your personal productivity gap, the more you will be respected by your supervisor.

Supervisors are rated by superiors on the size of their departmental productivity gaps. So they appreciate it when the relationships you build with co-workers result in a better team spirit and greater productivity. Sometimes they will take time to compliment you on your efforts in this area.

The key to a solid relationship with your new boss is open, two-way communication. This doesn't happen automatically. It needs to be built over a period of time and sustained. But how do you get started? What might you do the first week on the job? Following are three possibilities.

Possibility #1: THE SUPERVISOR COMMUNICATES WITH YOU. Chances are that your superior will initiate some form of communication, often during your first week. Take advantage of this opportunity to ask questions or discuss any problem related to your productivity (operation of machines, skills, etc.). If you sense that you are unusually slow, say so and wait for a feedback that may help you improve your productivity.

Possibility #2: YOU INITIATE COMMUNICATION. Not all good supervisors are outstanding as communicators. Some are often so busy they forget to discuss matters with new employees. Don't be afraid to walk up to your boss to ask how you are doing.

It is important for you to know. It is also important for your supervisor to know that you want to know. Any problems you do not communicate the first week will make things more difficult the second.

Possibility #3: WAIT UNTIL THE RIGHT OPPORTUNITY. It might have been a hectic week for your supervisor. You may need more time to prove you can handle things. In any case, if you do not communicate much with your superior the first week, make it a primary goal during your second week.

CO-WORKER RELATIONSHIPS

The best way to build a positive relationship with your supervisor is to build good working relationships with your fellow-workers.

When you do this you add to the harmony of the working environment and make a double contribution to departmental productivity. You contribute, and you make it easier for others to do the same!

How do you build strong relationships with co-workers? Here are three suggestions to get you started.

1. **BE A COMFORTABLE PERSON.** Unless you are friendly and communicate openly and frequently with your co-workers, you may make *them* feel uncomfortable. This, in turn, can lead to misinterpretation. Instead of the easy-to-know person you can be, co-workers may interpret you as stuffy, a loner, or someone who thinks he's too good for the job. Do not allow this to happen.

2. **ACCEPT ASSISTANCE GRACIOUSLY.** It may be necessary for you to learn important tasks from someone with far less education or a different background than you. In any case, go beyond the standard "thank you." For example, you might say: "You have been a terrific help," or "I really owe you one."

3. **PUT THE MUTUAL REWARD IDEA TO WORK.** Later on (after you fully develop your skills) there will be many ways you can repay your co-workers by chipping in when they need extra help. Your first week (if it seems appropriate) you might consider baking a cake or buying some doughnuts as a thank-you for those who helped you through your first days.

*YOU NEVER GET A SECOND CHANCE TO MAKE
A FIRST IMPRESSION*

THE THIRTY-DAY HUMILITY SCALE

Surveys show that the biggest mistake new employees make is to flaunt their education or previous experience in a new work environment. Nothing turns off co-workers and superiors faster than a know-it-all who does not appear willing to learn.

To help keep you from falling into this trap, you are invited to complete the following scale. Indicate whether you think the statement is true or false. Score yourself at the bottom of the page.

TRUE	FALSE	
_____	_____	1. No matter how much you know, your input will not be automatically accepted as valid when you start a new job.
_____	_____	2. The higher your academic background is, the easier the adjustment to your new position will be.
_____	_____	3. It's better to be modest in behavior than to make a humiliating mistake because you didn't listen and learn.
_____	_____	4. To have a good learning attitude even a PhD needs a degree of humility.
_____	_____	5. To become less assertive than usual is never a good idea on a new job.
_____	_____	6. Co-workers will be more impressed with your past achievements if they learn about them from someone else, rather than from you.
_____	_____	7. Experience is a great teacher.
_____	_____	8. All supervisors have had an abundance of formal education.
_____	_____	9. It is asking too much of new employees to play down their expertise until they have built strong relationships with others.
_____	_____	10. In the work environment, productivity is more important than previous educational achievements.

SCORE [ ]

ANSWERS: 1 T; 2 F; 3 T; 4 T; 5 F; 6 T; 7 T; 8 F; 9 F; 10 T.

It is up to each new employee to decide when and how to provide technical skills or expertise that they possess. Sometimes it is needed immediately. At other times, all it takes is a few days before it can be effectively introduced. Most of the time, it is best to learn from others and then weave your own ideas (and expertise) into your productivity. Whatever the situation, to antagonize others is counterproductive.

FIRST WEEK ASSESSMENT SCALE

This exercise is a personal progress report. It is designed to help you pinpoint areas of success or areas where renewed emphasis is needed. Complete this assessment only after you have been on your new job a full week. Check the appropriate box. Be totally honest with yourself.

	FULLY SATISFIED	PARTIALLY SATISFIED	NOT SATISFIED
Did I take advantage of learning opportunities?	☐	☐	☐
Did I avoid making too many first-week mistakes?	☐	☐	☐
How was my application of job skills?	☐	☐	☐
My grooming?	☐	☐	☐
My level of concentration?	☐	☐	☐
My success at remembering names?	☐	☐	☐
How were my first-week listening skills?	☐	☐	☐
Did my personal productivity improve?	☐	☐	☐
Did I make a good impression on my co-workers?	☐	☐	☐
On my supervisor?	☐	☐	☐

Based on my answers, I intend to concentrate on improving the following areas next week:

1. _____

2. _____

3. _____

4. _____

5. _____

WHAT DO I NEED TO LEARN NEXT WEEK?

Has your supervisor or sponsor given you any learning tasks? What have you observed that you will be required to learn in the future? What do you *want* to learn next week?

To demonstrate your initiative and stay ahead of what your supervisor expects you to learn, list those tasks you wish to become better at next week. List them in the order in which you want to learn them.

1. _____

2. _____

3. _____

4. _____

5. _____

Psychologically it is often motivating to reward yourself for reaching short-term learning goals. Write out a reward that you promise yourself (Dinner out? New article of clothing? Sporting event?) if you reach your goals next week.

MY REWARD BOX

WEEK TWO

MOVING AHEAD
WITH CONFIDENCE

Always take a job that is too big for you.
—Harry Emerson Fosdick

SECOND-WEEK PRODUCTIVITY

It is customary for new employees to use the second week on the job to get personal productivity as close to standard (or the average of other employees) as possible.

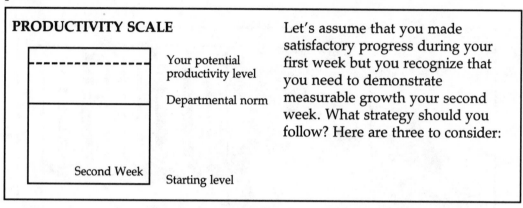

PRODUCTIVITY SCALE

Your potential productivity level

Departmental norm

Second Week

Starting level

Let's assume that you made satisfactory progress during your first week but you recognize that you need to demonstrate measurable growth your second week. What strategy should you follow? Here are three to consider:

Strategy #1: Go all out to get your personal productivity level up to that of your co-workers. If necessary, curtail your socialization. Be friendly and pleasant, but let your job concentration do the talking.

Strategy #2: Announce to co-workers that your goal for the week is to get your productivity up to their level. Do this in a good-natured way and suggest that they keep an eye on your progress. Let them know that suggestions from them are welcome!

Strategy #3: Silently concentrate on personal productivity but do not neglect human relations. Strive for balance between the two and, if necessary, give yourself an additional week to reach the level of your co-workers.

In some situations (where you are finding it easy to reach productivity standards) you might concentrate on human relations. This is a good approach when you realize you can surpass the productivity of others but you do not want them to feel threatened by your ability.

HOW TO HANDLE EMBARRASSING MOMENTS

Few things can be more embarrassing than to fail at something you have been trained to do well. For example, imagine the embarrassment of an English major who misspells a word in a letter the first week on the job. Or an accountant who makes a mistake in simple arithmetic.

Mistakes due to lack of experience can be embarrassing, too.

You might have to make change for customers when you've never made change before. Or you might be faced with equipment you've never used before.

> "Ten years ago I was accepted in a management training program by a chain of restaurants. My first assignment was to operate the cash register. A hostess was assigned to check me out, but I was more interested in her than her instructions. Result? I made so many dumb mistakes that I had to be retrained in front of everyone by the one person I was trying to impress—the manager."

Countless other mistakes can happen on any new job. One way to minimize mistakes is through self-training. Here are a few suggestions:

- Admit your lack of experience if you have not had the required training.
- Position yourself so you can both hear the trainer/teacher and see the mechanics involved. Ask questions.
- Ask to do a dry run for any new procedure.
- Do new tasks step by step at your own speed until you become comfortable.
- If necessary, accept more help.
- Do not be afraid to ask for retraining. Find out who you should approach to receive it.

Everyone makes mistakes. When it happens to you, keep your sense of humor. Learn to laugh at yourself, and others will respect you. The biggest mistake is to assume you know how to do something before you really do, so that you make the same mistake again and again. Making a mistake in your first week is expected. Making the same mistake the second and third week is not and will not enhance your image.

COPING WITH SKILL DEFICIENCIES

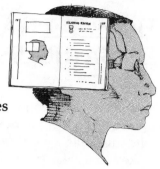

What happens if you draw a first assignment that requires a skill above your level of experience? The following suggestions should help:

> - Ask your supervisor for a "sponsor" to assist you in getting your skill level higher.
>
> - Cancel your plans for the next few nights so you can make improvements by staying late at work or practicing elsewhere.
>
> - Pay for some immediate tutoring (for example, at a local college campus).
>
> - Enroll in the first available class for more extensive upgrading.

It is a mistake to try and hide your skill level from others. Admitting you need help can often turn out to be an icebreaker with fellow employees. They may have been in the same position themselves earlier. Once you receive on-the-job assistance it is important to demonstrate that you have benefited and that your skill performance has improved. To strengthen relationships with those who have "bailed you out," wait for an opportunity to do something of importance for them so they fully understand how much you appreciated their help when you needed it the most.

It may be possible for your manager to arrange for you to upgrade your skills by arriving early or staying late. Asking if this is possible demonstrates a good learning attitude.

Upgrading a skill takes time. Make sure your other job responsibilities are not neglected. In fact, it may be possible to temporarily offset the lack of skill in one area by contributing more in another where you are proficient. Perhaps a trade-off with a co-worker could be arranged.

Give yourself thirty days to improve as many skills as possible. If you need more help, tell your supervisor what you are doing to improve your situation. Compensate for slow skill development by developing good human relations. It is your total contribution to the organization that will eventually be measured.

IMPROVING YOUR JOB SKILLS

Each job has its unique skill requirements. Some job skills (waitress, equipment operator, etc.) can be taught from scratch after one is employed. Most jobs, however, require a certain skill level before employment is offered (computer operator, carpenter, etc.). In all cases, new employees are required to either improve or adjust their existing skills.

COMPANY SOURCES:

Supervisor. Your boss is responsible for your training and job performance. She or he may or may not give you the training you need. Some supervisors are outstanding instructors. Good luck!

Sponsor. It is a common and good practice for a supervisor to assign a sponsor (co-worker) who will train and guide you through your first weeks.

Training. If you were fortunate enough to receive orientation training, it probably came from the human resources department. Check to see what other training is available and if your organization may provide correspondence courses, self-help books, etc.*

CAMPUS SOURCES:

Regular Classes. Credit classes dealing with your needed job skills may be available.

Learning Centers. Most campuses have learning centers where remedial classes and tutoring are available. Check it out.

Continuing Education Programs. Most colleges have noncredit, short-unit skill programs that might fit your needs and off-work hours.

Trade Schools. Many trade schools have open-ended skill programs where you can enroll anytime and finish at your own speed.

SELF-HELP:

Equipment Suppliers. Computer manufacturers often provide training manuals and software to teach their system or program.

Libraries. Libraries can often provide computers, videos, and self-help manuals and books.*

Whatever local sources may be available, it is the responsibility of the new employee to bring his or her skills up to standard and beyond.

*For an excellent list of self-study titles, see the back of this book.

YOUR COMMUNICATION STYLE

It is vital that you speak up clearly and concisely in your new job. It is also important that any forms, notes, or memos be written in your best penmanship, printed, or typed. People need to hear and understand what you mean. If your English is weak (perhaps a new second language), seek assistance.

The manner or style in which you communicate may be different from your normal style and from the way you will communicate later. Why is this? In most cases your approach will be conservative because you feel this style will help you win the acceptance of co-workers. Later you can relax and communicate in your own way.

How communicative should you be at first? Just enough to be friendly and get your tasks done? If you are not open, will people feel you are withdrawn and hard to know? What is enough communication but not too much for your first days?

Many factors are involved (especially the kind of environment you walk into), but here are two styles you might consider on a temporary basis:

Style #1: Remain more quiet than usual. Concentrate on the work. Be very polite. Ask questions only when necessary. Communicate primarily with your attitude and job performance instead of with your voice. Do not be embarrassed if you appear nervous.

Style #2: Be modestly assertive. Call people by their first names if appropriate. Speak with confidence but be careful not to dominate conversations. Show your positive learning attitude by asking more questions than necessary. Be friendly and open. When appropriate, get others to laugh.

Show your preference for style #1 or #2 by answering the following questions.

	Style #1	Style #2
As a long-time employee, which style would you react to best in a newcomer?	☐	☐
Which of the two styles comes closest to your natural style?	☐	☐
Which style would help a new employee make the most progress in the first thirty days?	☐	☐
As a supervisor, which style would you prefer a new employee to use?	☐	☐

The above exercise is designed to get you thinking about how important communication will be to your success during the first weeks. Your best strategy, of course, is the one that falls within your "comfort zone" and will build the best relationships with others. You decide!

TEASING AND TESTING

To be an outsider one day and an insider the next without a little teasing or testing may be asking too much. Co-workers often enjoy a joke at the expense of the newcomer. Some supervisors like to see how a new employee handles a difficult assignment.

Teasing is when co-workers have a little fun at your expense.

> When Judy reported to work her second week, she was told by a co-worker to fax a copy of her resume (the one she used to get her job) to headquarters in Chicago. Judy did this without question and the reply from Chicago was ''looks interesting, suggest she visit the office for an interview if she plans a trip to Chicago.'' This response brought a good laugh!

Because Judy was able to laugh about it herself, her relationship with co-workers took a giant step forward. The laughter was, in a sense, a form of acceptance.

Testing is a more serious matter, and it is important to know the difference between the two. Where teasing is usually harmless, testing may indicate resentment, jealousy, or even fear.

> When Harold was assigned to Mr. G for training, things didn't go well. He was given tasks to perform without being told how to do them. Then he was reprimanded for being slow. After two days, Harold knew something was seriously wrong, so he walked into Mr. G's office seeking an explanation. To his surprise, Mr. G quickly apologized, saying: ''I thought that you were sent to replace me, and I was going to be out of a job. I decided to give you a bad time, hoping you would throw in the sponge. But I just learned I have been promoted to a new job. So I will drop everything now and give you all the training you need. Sorry.''

Sometimes a new employee is tested by a co-worker for unexplained, personal reasons. At other times testing may occur when a co-worker feels you are getting breaks she or he did not receive as a new employee. If, as a new employee, you find the testing is persistent (not just a temporary reaction), two actions are recommended. First, confront the person who keeps testing you and ask why. Second, discuss the matter with your supervisor. If it is the supervisor who is doing the testing, and you judge it to be unfair, you have no choice but to discuss the matter with the supervisor. If the testing doesn't stop, you should talk to his or her superior.

PROTOCOL

Protocol means those courtesies, manners, and procedures considered proper in dealing with people within an organization. Protocol describes the unwritten rules co-workers and managers expect you to follow in certain situations. In most cases, you learn protocol after you have been on the job awhile.

Such matters as the length of coffee breaks, the number of sick days allowed, and similar rules are covered in employee manuals and can be learned quickly. But much protocol is not written out. For example, in most organizations it is a mistake to go over the head of your supervisor to discuss problems of importance to your department. It violates protocol because it undermines the supervisor's authority.

The following list describes areas where sensitivity is required. Check any item that you feel would apply to your new job. I plan to be sensitive when:

- [ ] Asking questions of my superiors
- [ ] Setting up a communications session with my boss
- [ ] Keeping my business and personal life separated
- [ ] Talking in a negative manner about fellow employees
- [ ] Discussing business details in a crowded elevator
- [ ] Using first names
- [ ] Speaking or laughing in a loud voice that disturbs others
- [ ] Telling jokes or stories that might offend others
- [ ] Eavesdropping
- [ ] Dressing in a manner that consistently distracts others from their productivity
- [ ] _____

Protocol applies to delicate matters in which you have a choice of behavior. You can act in a courteous, sensitive manner, or in a way that might embarrass others and make good relationships difficult. Of course, protocol is just as important after being on the job for a while as it is during your first few days. The big difference is that more people will watch your behavior more closely at the beginning.

IMPROVING WORK HABITS

Some typical bad habits are listed below. Place a check next to those you want to avoid.

☐ Keeping a messy desk or work station

☐ Turning in a poorly written report

☐ Doing a poor job of personal time management

☐ Not being well groomed (dirty fingernails, uncombed hair, unshined shoes)

☐ Making or receiving too many personal telephone calls

☐ Presenting a negative attitude to others when you really feel positive inside

☐ Not taking good care of company equipment

☐ Being late for work or for appointments

☐ Making promises that you can't keep

☐ Putting quantity ahead of quality

If you are starting your first career job after graduating from school, you have a golden opportunity to form good habits. The same is true if you are entering the workplace after an absence. But if you built an inventory of bad habits in your previous job, you have a major challenge. You must leave your bad habits behind and learn new ones.

Either way, here are three reminders:

- It is much easier to eliminate bad work habits at the time you enter a new environment.

- In your desire to be accepted by co-workers, do not pick up their bad habits to add to your own.

- If you have a habit or mannerism that irritates others in your personal life, it will probably be twice as offensive to co-workers.

Developing good work habits is the professional way to go!

CASE #2: UNPREPARED

It is Saturday morning and Dean is reflecting back on his second week with Ace Tech. Everyone has been helpful and friendly and Dean feels proud to be associated with such an impressive group of professionals. But he is deeply concerned over what happened just before he left work Friday. His superior, Jane Shafer, called him into her office and said he would replace Alice Redley as head of the accounts receivable department starting Monday morning.

Although Dean is an accounting major with computer skills, he's worried that Ms. Shafer may be assuming he is more qualified and experienced than he really is. Without meaning to, she may be leading him to failure. Dean is not familiar with the types of computers used, or the accounts receivable system at Ace. As far as he can tell, when Monday morning arrives he will be on his own.

Please list what you think Dean should do over the weekend to better prepare himself for Monday morning.

_____

_____

_____

_____

What should Dean do upon arriving at work Monday morning?

_____

_____

_____

_____

Compare your thoughts with those of the author by turning to page 64.

SECOND WEEK ASSESSMENT SCALE

This exercise is designed to help you evaluate your progress after two weeks on your new job. Check the appropriate box. Honesty with yourself will guarantee you a better future!

	FULLY SATISFIED	PARTIALLY SATISFIED	NOT SATISFIED
How is my learning progress after two weeks?	☐	☐	☐
How is my progress in building good relationships with co-workers?	☐	☐	☐
How am I doing in closing my personal productivity gap?	☐	☐	☐
How do I rate my patience with others?	☐	☐	☐
Am I building a strong relationship with my supervisor?	☐	☐	☐
How do I feel about my personal confidence?	☐	☐	☐
What about my ability to relax and enjoy my work?	☐	☐	☐
Do I remain positive in all situations?	☐	☐	☐
How are my health and energy level?	☐	☐	☐
How do I feel about myself?	☐	☐	☐

Based on my answers, I intend to concentrate on making improvements in the following areas next week:

1. _____
2. _____
3. _____
4. _____
5. _____

WHAT DO I NEED TO LEARN NEXT WEEK?

What success did you achieve in reaching your learning goals last week? Did you reward yourself as planned? If circumstances were such that you weren't able to learn everything you planned, please try again next week. Feel free to add any learning tasks you listed last week (but were unable to learn) and also list some new ones. In addition, please add any learning tasks you have been assigned by others.

1. _____

2. _____

3. _____

4. _____

5. _____

What reward will you give yourself if you reach all your goals next week?

REWARD BOX

WEEK THREE

STRENGTHENING RELATIONSHIPS

> Work is what you do so that sometime you
> won't have to do it anymore.
>
> —Alfred Polgar

THIRD WEEK PRODUCTIVITY

Chances are good that by now your productivity is up to your, and your supervisor's, expectations. If it isn't, you should initiate a conversation with your supervisor so that retraining or other adjustments can be made.

Let's assume, however, that you are up to the standard of your co-workers, and you feel that you can start to move ahead of that standard. In other words, you can continue to close the gap between your present productivity and your potential.

How should you go about doing this?

Carefully is the key word, because you want to continue strengthening relationships while you improve your productivity. You want your extra productivity to inspire others to do better themselves—not to turn them against you because they feel you are showing them up.

> When Sid knew his productivity was at least average in the department, he decided to turn on the steam to gain the attention of his supervisor and, hopefully, set himself up for a quick promotion. Result? Sid turned his co-workers against him and his supervisor found it necessary to give him his "teamwork approach to productivity" lecture.

Many new employees fail to see that they also contribute to productivity when they make it more comfortable for their co-workers to produce. Sid, despite his high potential, did not sense the big picture until his superior came down on him.

Don't let this happen to you!

Your strategy should be to move your personal productivity higher in such a way that your fellow employees support your efforts and are motivated to follow. This is the only way you can make your maximum contribution to your department.

It is also the best strategy to use in preparing yourself for a future position as a supervisor. Good luck!

WHAT IF YOU DRAW A DIFFICULT SUPERVISOR?

Just as there are problem co-workers, there are also difficult supervisors. Some are excessively demanding. Some have little patience. Others find it difficult to communicate. Regardless of the kind of supervisor you draw, it is vital that you build the best possible relationship with this person. How do you do this? There are two major factors for immediate consideration:

1. **REACT TO THE MANAGEMENT STYLE OF YOUR SUPERVISOR,** not to her or his personality. All supervisors develop a unique way of operating. Your challenge is to adjust to this style and ignore individual traits or mannerisms (voice, expressions, physical features, manner of dress, peculiarities). In other words, look past your supervisor's personality to what she or he is trying to accomplish.

2. **CONCENTRATE ON PRODUCTIVITY AND CO-WORKER RELATIONSHIPS** as you learn to work in harmony with your supervisor. Who knows—your supervisor may be staying neutral until it is known how productive you are and how effectively you work with others. Above all, do not let fellow employees turn you against a supervisor who may eventually be your greatest supporter.

In addition, the following tips are suggested:

- Don't expect a perfect supervisor.

- Remember that supervisors are human and sometimes have rough days.

- Select the right time to ask questions.

- Refuse to allow a small matter turn into a major issue.

- Don't go above your supervisor's head, except as a last resort.

- If you make a mistake, tell your boss yourself. He or she should not hear about it from others.

It is far better to take time to figure out how to build a good relationship with a boss, than to judge him or her too quickly. Take it easy and give your superior a chance to know just how professional you really can be!

CASE #3

CASE #3: CHOICE

On Monday morning after two weeks on the job, Joyce was invited into the office of her supervisor, Ms. Crane. Tense about the purpose of the meeting, Joyce was relieved when Ms. Crane paid her a sincere compliment and told her that the employee Joyce was hired to replace was returning from leave sooner than expected. She told Joyce not to worry because two other supervisors had requested her services. Best of all, Joyce can have her choice between the two assignments.

Department A is supervised by Mr. King, a long-term employee. Department A has the reputation of promoting more employees into better jobs than any other department. Mr. King is considered an outstanding teacher. On the other hand, he is highly authoritarian. In fact, he runs such a tight ship that his employee turnover is higher than that of any other supervisor in the company.

Department B is supervised by Ms. Joy, a young manager recently out of college. This department has the reputation of getting high productivity from people, and they seem to have fun doing it. Many workers envy those who work in Ms. Joy's department. On the other hand, no one from her department has been promoted in the two years since Ms. Joy became manager.

If you were Joyce, which department would you choose? Why?

_____

_____

_____

_____

_____

_____

_____

_____

_____

_____

_____

To compare your answer with that of the author, turn to page 64.

REINFORCING RELATIONSHIPS

After a couple of weeks on the job, you have had an opportunity to build a few new and rewarding relationships. Some were probably easier to build than others. You may not have been successful in all directions. This is natural, because some people are more reserved than others. And a few people present a special challenge because they do not give their support quickly to any newcomer. The good news is that once you build a good working relationship with these more reserved colleagues, it is likely to be a meaningful, lasting one.

Please list below the names of those co-workers you wish to build strong relationships with but with whom you have had little success so far.

1. _____   3. _____

2. _____   4. _____

How are you going to develop relationships with these special co-workers and improve your relationships with others? Here are four suggestions:

1. Continue to maintain your productivity and your image as a serious, professional worker.

2. Be generous with thank-you's. Comments like these are appreciated: "Thanks for making my first weeks easier." "You have been a great help to me. Thanks." "Without your assistance my adjustment here would have been a lot less fun. Thanks a million."

3. Continue to ask for advice. Asking for advice is an excellent way to improve a relationship. "Could you tell me how to learn new features of the word processing software?" "I've mastered most of my tasks but I am still having trouble with the reduction machine. Could you check me out to see what I am doing wrong?"

4. Pay more compliments. Don't wait any longer to pay sincere compliments, even to those who are holding back a little. "I wish I was as good on the telephone as you." "I'll never learn to match your speed." "I sure appreciate your professionalism. I hope you don't mind if I try some of your techniques."

AVOIDING PERSONAL JOB STRESS

When specialists talk about job stress they are usually referring to the excessive pressure that some jobs create. This stress can lead to the mental and emotional exhaustion known as job burnout.

It is also possible to create unnecessary stress for yourself when you are in a new job. Sometimes new employees try so hard to succeed that they wear down their immune systems and catch cold or develop other stress-related illnesses.

How can you prevent this from happening?

Here are three suggestions:

1. **Regulate your work tempo.** When you move into a new environment, it is easy to succumb to the pressures that surround you. When you permit this to happen, your job performance goes down instead of up. Make sure you take all of the breaks coming to you and resist working beyond scheduled times. Resist pressure to speed up. Keep regular hours off the job for the first few weeks. Exercise on a daily basis. The phrase ''one day at a time'' will never have more meaning to you than during this time.

2. **Learn to perform on a daily step-up pattern.** Each new day on the job, pick up your tempo a little without getting too excited and overdoing it. Learn to do one job at a time so you won't get frustrated trying to go in too many directions at once. Despite the many demands on you, develop your own pace. It may be necessary to discuss your progress with your supervisor so you are not forced to take on too many responsibilities too soon.

3. **Within limits, kid around a little.** As a new employee, you will need the safety valve of laughter even more than others. Relax and enjoy your co-workers when the time is right. Initiate humor when it's appropriate. Allow the stress that does accumulate within you to escape.

THE THREE C'S OF OFFICE POLITICS

When people work together, there will naturally be a variety of values, standards, and cultural differences. In some environments these differences manifest themselves in the form of office politics. When this happens, workers sometimes spar off against each other, and the harmony desired by management disappears.

As a new member, you can be caught up in the winds and tides of politics, and your career has the potential of being damaged. How do you avoid this? How can you stay clear? It may help to know about the three C's of office politics: camps, cliques, and critics.

CAMPS

Without knowing it, you may walk into a work environment that is divided into two or more camps. One camp might be pro-management, the other not. One camp might be pro-union, the other not. Or it is possible that one camp rallies around one worker, another camp around another. The danger, of course, is that you may be in the middle and intimidated into making a choice. What is the solution? Stay clear and chart a course down the middle.

CLIQUES

A clique can be viewed as a small camp that does not have any opposition. Most cliques are composed of a small circle of people who like to stick together. This can be seen during breaks. Cliques often appear exclusive or snobbish to other workers. Your career will be better off if you do not join a clique, especially at first. Reason? Because the moment you join you are playing favorites. Your challenge is to get along equally with *all* employees. Here again, stay clear and chart a course so that both clique members and others respect you.

CRITICS

All organizations have a few critics on the payroll. Many are experienced people who have sidetracked themselves into a dead-end job. They love to convert newcomers to their negative views. How do you deal with a critic? Listen, be polite, but don't be taken in. And, above all, do not let yourself be over-identified with a critic.

Keep the three C's in mind as you try to build good, sound, healthy working relationships with all the people in your environment.

CASE #4

CASE #4: ABSENTEEISM

After a wonderful scuba-diving trip over the weekend, Kelly woke up Monday morning with a high temperature and feeling miserable. It was only her third week on the new job (which she loves), but she knew she had to call in sick so adjustments could be made and others could pick up the slack. Kelly also called in sick Tuesday and Wednesday. Sensing she might be creating a problem for herself if she missed any more days, she went to work Thursday and struggled through until the weekend.

When she reports to work the next Monday (almost fully recovered), everyone, including her supervisor, is friendly and sympathetic. So much so, that she relaxes and talks about all the fun she had on her scuba trip and neglects to thank others for picking up the slack. Although nothing is said, Kelly begins to notice some distancing between her and her co-workers. They seem less eager to help her. Her supervisor appears more demanding.

Do you think Kelly's absenteeism damaged her career start? Why and where has the damage occurred? Can she repair the damage? How?

_____

_____

_____

_____

_____

_____

_____

_____

_____

_____

See page 64 to compare your answer with that of the author.

THIRD WEEK ASSESSMENT SCALE

Complete this assessment after you have been on the job three weeks.

	FULLY SATISFIED	PARTIALLY SATISFIED	NOT SATISFIED
Have I increased my personal productivity to my best level?	☐	☐	☐
What about the quality of my work?	☐	☐	☐
How are my human relations skills?	☐	☐	☐
How is my on-time and absentee record?	☐	☐	☐
Am I maintaining a good visual image?	☐	☐	☐
Have I reduced the number of my mistakes at a fast enough pace?	☐	☐	☐
How about my verbal skills?	☐	☐	☐
Have I succeeded in not showing a negative attitude?	☐	☐	☐
Have I taken full advantage of all opportunities?	☐	☐	☐
How do I rate my professional growth and image so far?	☐	☐	☐

Based on my answers, I intend to concentrate on improving the following areas next week:

1. _____

2. _____

3. _____

4. _____

5. _____

WHAT DO I NEED TO LEARN NEXT WEEK?

Your thirty days will soon be up, so it's time to concentrate on learning any tasks that are still a problem for you. Are there a few tasks you have neglected? Do you need to retrain yourself (or get some special help) on a learning goal that is giving you trouble? List below those remaining things (operating a machine, completing a special report, etc.) that you wish to learn next week.

1. _____

2. _____

3. _____

4. _____

5. _____

If you feel really good about your learning progress over the past three weeks and you feel confident you can accomplish most of the goals listed above, shouldn't you go overboard a little and promise yourself a special reward?

REWARD BOX

WEEK FOUR

IMPROVING YOUR PROFESSIONALISM

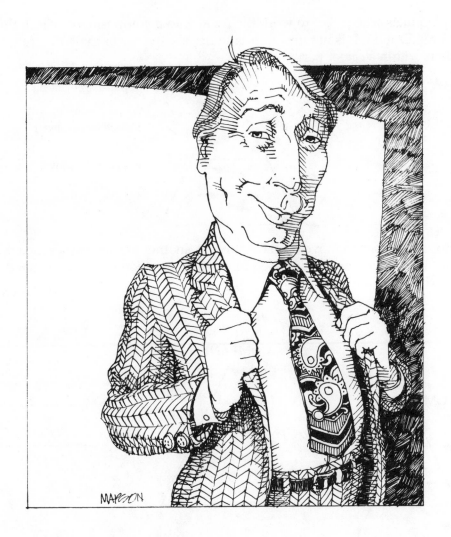

> Actually, I'm an overnight success. But it took twenty years.
>
> —Monty Hall

CAREER COUNTDOWN

Whatever your new job or new assignment happens to be, it should be considered as a launching pad to help you reach long-term career goals. In this respect a job is never just a job—it is an opportunity.

For individuals who prefer to work their way into better positions within the same organization, it is not uncommon to occupy twenty or more different positions within a career period.

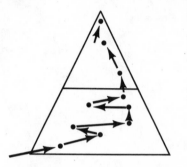

Top management

Middle management

Lower management

For those who elect to move from one firm to another as they zigzag their way to the top, their moves are made based upon the reputation they have created behind them.

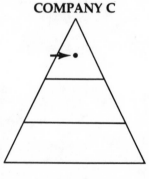

COMPANY C

COMPANY B

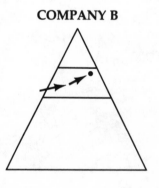

COMPANY A

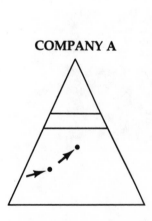

Either way, you have much more at stake than the position you occupy when you start out. Everything you learn can be used later on in your career in more demanding positions!

CASE #5

CASE #5: PREMATURE?

As far as he can tell, Jack has made a smooth and satisfactory adjustment to his new job. Although there has been little communication with him, his supervisor seems happy. Two co-workers have ignored Jack, but the others haven't given him any trouble. Best of all, Jack has found it easy to get his job skills and productivity up to par. All in all, it has been a good three weeks.

While driving home one evening, Jack started thinking about his possibilities of becoming a supervisor with his firm. ''After all,'' he said to himself, ''if I can make so much progress in such a short period of time, what is to hold me back? I think I'll make an appointment tomorrow with my supervisor. I'll get his advice on what steps I need to take to qualify myself for his job or a similar one in another department.''

How do you think Jack's supervisor would answer? Please write out your response below.

_____

_____

_____

_____

_____

_____

_____

_____

_____

_____

_____

To compare your answer with that of the author, turn to page 64.

MISGIVINGS

Interviews indicate that almost all new employees have down periods—a sudden flurry of doubts about whether they made the right decision in accepting their new job or assignment. Like after buying a new car, a temporary wave of remorse may occur. New employees frequently ask themselves questions like these:

> What am I doing here?
> Am I with the right organization?
> Can I learn all they are throwing at me?
> Did I spend all that time in college for this?

Misgivings are natural and to be expected. They are part of the adjustment period. Sometimes a simple little incident will trigger a down period.

> Norma was sailing into her new job with confidence. Then one day, after completing a difficult customer transaction, she noticed her supervisor watching her with an air of dissatisfaction. That night Norma had trouble sleeping. But the next day the supervisor, sensing what might have occurred, told Norma that she handled things extremely well and that he was actually upset with the customer (a known complainer). Norma's confidence quickly returned.

However, most doubts occur when new employees start to fear that they cannot bring their skills up high enough to hold their positions. They are overwhelmed by how much they have to learn and temporarily forget that they have plenty of time to learn it. Usually all it takes is a lunch break or a good night's sleep, and the misgivings disappear. Here are three tips that can help speed up the confidence restoration process:

- If you start to feel the job may be too much for you, concentrate on productivity.
- If you feel rejected by co-workers, ask the one you respect the most to tell you what you may be doing wrong.
- Keep reminding yourself that Rome wasn't built in a day and that you have time to improve.

BALANCING PRODUCTIVITY AND HUMAN RELATIONS

Your primary goal during your first thirty days should be to achieve the best possible balance between high productivity and good human relations. It is a goal that should remain with you throughout your career.

In the diagram below, notice that the employee in the middle has increased his or her productivity to above average while at the same time establishing a strong relationship with the supervisor (vertical relationship) and good working relationships with two co-workers (horizontal relationships). Keeping the vertical and horizontal relationships at high levels, and in balance, is the key to career success.

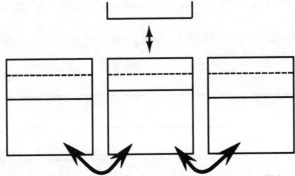

Once you achieve a good balance, your future challenge will be to improve and maintain it. Here are three suggestions:

- *It is as dangerous to become sloppy with human relationships as it is with your job performance.* Keep reminding yourself that you contribute to departmental productivity in two ways—what you do, and what others do because you are a team player.

- *Do not resent others because you seem to carry more departmental productivity than they do.* You may be more ambitious than your fellow employees, or you may have received better training elsewhere, or your potential may be higher.

- *Helping others reach their productivity potential can mean as much to your career as doing it yourself.* As you have learned from those who assisted you, a great way to build a lasting relationship with a co-worker is to help that person succeed. Helping others is an excellent way to promote your career.

Become professional!
Stay professional!
Enjoy being professional!

CASE #6

56

CASE #6: STYLE

During his first few weeks with Ace Tech, Brad attempted to be a highly visible new employee with an unusual capacity to produce. His style was assertive but professional, confident but sensitive. His attitude was positive and he was fun to be around. One of the old-timers made this statement about Brad: "He is typical of the new breed. You like him because of his type A personality, but you know he isn't going to waste any time on his way to the top."

During his first thirty days with Ace Tech, Sid chose to keep a low profile. He wanted to be comfortable and easy to know. Sid made a special effort to help others. He listened carefully before jumping in with suggestions. Sid worked hard to build sound relations with both co-workers and superiors. One fellow employee said this of Sid: "He is really a nice guy. In my opinion, he will eventually make a strong employee. I like his style. He has my support."

Who, in your opinion, has made the most progress in thirty days, Brad or Sid? Who has been the most professional?

_____

_____

_____

_____

_____

_____

_____

_____

_____

_____

Turn to page 64 to compare your answer with that of the author.

FOURTH WEEK ASSESSMENT

**TALKING THINGS OVER WITH
A FRIEND, SPOUSE, MENTOR, OR ADVISOR**

Although you may have been sharing your experiences informally with friends, now that you are completing your first month it might be smart to talk over your total experience over more seriously with a significant other.

Have things turned out the way you figured?
Has this book helped? How?
What has happened to your image both on and off the job?
Do you have more confidence than when you started your job?
What would you do differently the next time you start a new job or move into a new environment?
Do you consider yourself a stronger person now?
Has there been any permanent improvement in your learning attitude? Your attitude in general?
If the person (or persons) you select to talk with should start a new job, would you suggest using this book?

Talking over these questions with the right person could help reinforce what you have learned, and could help you crystallize your thoughts for the future.

In addition to talking things over, you might enjoy testing yourself on what you have learned. If so, complete the self-quiz on the following page.

58

DEMONSTRATE YOUR PROGRESS

For each statement below, put a check under True or False.

TRUE	FALSE	
____	____	1. What you have learned on your new job about being a more comfortable person to meet will probably not help you in other social situations.
____	____	2. Most career professionals would find it embarrassing to take notes in front of others.
____	____	3. Although there is always a gap between one's productivity level and one's potential, the smaller the gap the better.
____	____	4. It is possible to compensate for a lack of formal education and experience by having a superior learning attitude.
____	____	5. As a new employee, the best way to build good relationships with co-workers is to make sure your personal productivity is far above average during your first few days.
____	____	6. Practicing good human relations is the best way to overcome deficiencies in productive skills.
____	____	7. New employees who have come from another job have an advantage over first-time employees when it comes to establishing good work habits.
____	____	8. You should react to the personality of the supervisor and not to his or her management style.
____	____	9. Knowing the three C's of office politics reminds the new employee to play it safe and build good relationships with *all* co-workers.
____	____	10. In the beginning of a new experience, humility and a good learning attitude go together.

SCORE [ ]

ANSWERS: 1: False (It should be a big help). 2: False (Just the opposite). 3: True. 4: True. 5: False (Any increase in productivity should be accompanied by some human relation efforts). 6: False (But human relations can help until the deficiency is corrected). 7: False (Those who come from other jobs usually have bad habits that need correcting). 8: False. 9: True. 10: True.

FINAL REVIEW

Those who speak most of progress measure it by quantity and not by quality.
—George Santayana

BE TRUE TO YOUR FUTURE!

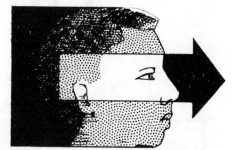

Whatever your experience has been in the past few weeks, two primary learning goals remain.

Learning Goal #1: It is vital that you sit down with your superior to discuss your strengths and weaknesses. Evaluation forms are provided on the next two pages. Please give your manager his or her copy in advance, so it will be completed when your meeting occurs.

In completing your form, you may wish to look back through this book (especially the assessment pages) to get a better fix on your learning progress.

When you meet with your supervisor, try to enjoy the process. Pay attention to suggestions you receive. Ask to review the supervisor's evaluation form in detail to make sure you know his or her thoughts about all phases of your performance.

Learning Goal #2: What kinds of training will you need in the future? Should you complete more formal training? How much can you continue to learn on the job? Will you be able to maintain your professional learning attitude as your career progresses?

To assist you in answering these and similar questions, complete the exercise "Consolidating Your Gains" on page 63.

THIRTY-DAY EVALUATION
EMPLOYEE'S COPY

This appraisal form is designed to be a significant part of *Your First Thirty Days*. (It does not replace other organizational performance appraisals.)

There are two copies of this form. The copy on this page should be completed by you. The copy on the next page (or a copy of it) should be completed by your supervisor. You and your supervisor should compare answers to measure the progress you have made and to discuss openly what can be done for your future growth. The experience should be positive and productive for both you and your supervisor.

In evaluating your performance, please circle the number most applicable. A 10, 9, or 8 is highly acceptable. A 7, 6, 5, or 4 is acceptable. A 3 or less is not acceptable.

	Highly Acceptable	Acceptable	Not Acceptable
Contribution to productivity during the first thirty days	10 9 8	7 6 5 4	3 2 1
Quality of relationships with co-workers	10 9 8	7 6 5 4	3 2 1
Skill improvement demonstrated	10 9 8	7 6 5 4	3 2 1
Absenteeism	10 9 8	7 6 5 4	3 2 1
Attitude	10 9 8	7 6 5 4	3 2 1
Willingness to learn	10 9 8	7 6 5 4	3 2 1
Communication skills	10 9 8	7 6 5 4	3 2 1
Professional image	10 9 8	7 6 5 4	3 2 1
Potential for growth	10 9 8	7 6 5 4	3 2 1
Participation as a team member	10 9 8	7 6 5 4	3 2 1

TOTAL SCORE [   ]

_____
Signature of Employee

THIRTY-DAY EVALUATION
SUPERVISOR'S COPY

Employee's name _____

This appraisal form is designed to be a significant part of *Your First Thirty Days*. (It does not replace other organizational performance appraisals.)

There are two copies of this form. This copy should be completed by the supervisor. Another copy will be completed by the employee. Both parties should then compare answers to measure the progress the employee has made and to discuss openly what can be done for his or her future growth. The experience should be positive and productive for both the supervisor and the employee.

In evaluating the employee's performance, please circle the number most applicable. A 10, 9, or 8 is highly acceptable. A 7, 6, 5, or 4 is acceptable. A 3 or less is not acceptable.

	Highly Acceptable	Acceptable	Not Acceptable
Contribution to productivity during the first thirty days	10 9 8	7 6 5 4	3 2 1
Quality of relationships with co-workers	10 9 8	7 6 5 4	3 2 1
Skill improvement demonstrated	10 9 8	7 6 5 4	3 2 1
Absenteeism	10 9 8	7 6 5 4	3 2 1
Attitude	10 9 8	7 6 5 4	3 2 1
Willingness to learn	10 9 8	7 6 5 4	3 2 1
Communication skills	10 9 8	7 6 5 4	3 2 1
Professional image	10 9 8	7 6 5 4	3 2 1
Potential for growth	10 9 8	7 6 5 4	3 2 1
Participation as a team member	10 9 8	7 6 5 4	3 2 1

TOTAL SCORE ☐

_____
Signature of Supervisor

CONSOLIDATING YOUR GAINS

In your first thirty days on the job, your knowledge should have expanded. Most of what you have learned has probably come from on-the-job experience. But you also gained knowledge, principles, and techniques from other sources.

How can you organize, consolidate, and prioritize what you have learned so it will mean more to you in the future?

Listed below are ten areas of concentration. If you decide which areas you made the most progress in, you will know where you excel. If you locate a few areas where you need extra growth to enhance your career, you will know where to concentrate your learning in the future.

Read all ten areas, then write the number 1 in the box where you feel you excel most. Write the number 2 in the box next to the area that comes next, and continue until you have written a 10 where you need the most help.

☐ Communications: all aspects (with superiors, co-workers, family, friends)

☐ Job skills: staying ahead of others in job competencies

☐ Human relations: building strong relationships with co-workers, superiors, customers, etc.

☐ Productivity: keeping personal productivity close to my potential and above the norm

☐ Self-management: making the best use of time, preventing burnout, balancing home and career, management of personal finances, etc.

☐ Attitude: being able to stay positive during stressful times; bouncing back quickly

☐ Image: maintaining a professional image in all of my career contacts

☐ Management skills: Do I aspire to a career in management? Do I have potential? What training have I had?

☐ Quality: Do I maintain the highest possible standards of excellence?

☐ Confidence: Am I sufficiently assertive or do I back away from confrontations?

For future growth, you should concentrate on the areas you designated as 6, 7, 8, 9, and 10.

ANSWERS TO CASES

CASE #1: RESCUE. It would appear that Ethel may have been rejected by co-workers and is getting back at them by trying to turn Patti against them. Patti needs to take time to make her own assessment of her co-workers. If she and Ethel become too close too soon, then others in the department may not give Patti a chance to know them. Patti needs to get to know everyone on an equal basis. She should tell Ethel she is too busy for after-work refreshments and that she will see Ethel tomorrow. A close relationship with Ethel may do Patti more harm than good.

CASE #2: UNPREPARED. Dean should go to the local library (or use texts he retained from college) to review accounts receivable. If possible, he should also spend some time with the kind of computer he will be using. On Monday morning Dean should arrive early and ask Ms. Shafer for a ''sponsor'' to teach him the ropes. If this isn't possible, he should ask those in the department for help and assistance.

CASE #3: CHOICE. Joyce should get as much additional information from Ms. Crane as possible. In fact, her advice could be crucial to the choice Joyce makes, because she has had a chance to observe Joyce at work for two weeks. If Joyce decides learning more and getting promoted sooner is more important than being in a happy environment, she should go with Mr. King. On the other hand, happy employees are often better motivated. Ms. Joy's style as a supervisor might act as a model for Joyce, and this might enhance her career more than going with Mr. King.

CASE #4: ABSENTEEISM. It may be unfair, but being absent within the first thirty days of a new job is usually more damaging than it would be later on. This is because the new employee has yet to pay her dues, and may still be a question mark in the minds of others. Kelly compounded the problem by talking about her fun weekend and by not thanking others for helping with the workload. The damage has been to Kelly's image as a responsible person. She can repair the damage, but it will take time.

CASE #5: PREMATURE? Jack's performance may have been enough to get him off to a fair start. But he has underestimated what he needs to be a successful employee, let alone a manager. Jack has not taken full advantage of his learning opportunities during the first three weeks, and it shows in his attitude.

CASE #6: STYLE. In the author's view, it is a toss-up between Brad and Sid. In some environments, Brad would make more progress. In other environments, Sid would come out ahead. There is less risk to Sid's style, because his lower-key approach is less apt to turn others against him. Also, if Sid stays in the same department, he may pass Brad because he may have stronger support from co-workers.

NOTES

FOR OTHER FIFTY-MINUTE SELF-STUDY BOOKS
SEE ORDER FORM AT THE BACK OF THE BOOK.

NOTES

THE FIFTY-MINUTE SERIES

Quantity	Title	Code #	Price	Amount
	MANAGEMENT TRAINING			
	Successful Negotiation	09-2	$7.95	
	Personal Performance Contracts	12-2	$7.95	
	Team Building	16-5	$7.95	
	Effective Meeting Skills	33-5	$7.95	
	An Honest Day's Work	39-4	$7.95	
	Managing Disagreement Constructively	41-6	$7.95	
	Training Managers To Train	43-2	$7.95	
	The Fifty-Minute Supervisor	58-0	$7.95	
	Leadership Skills For Women	62-9	$7.95	
	Problem Solving & Decision Making	63-7	$7.95	
	Coaching & Counseling For Supervisors	68-8	$7.95	
	Management Dilemmas: A Guide to Business Ethics	69-6	$7.95	
	Understanding Organizational Change	71-8	$7.95	
	Project Management	75-0	$7.95	
	Managing Organizational Change	80-7	$7.95	
	Managing A Diverse Workforce	85-8	$7.95	
	PERSONNEL TRAINING & HUMAN RESOURCE MANAGEMENT			
	Effective Performance Appraisals	11-4	$7.95	
	Quality Interviewing	13-0	$7.95	
	Personal Counseling	14-9	$7.95	
	Job Performance and Chemical Dependency	27-0	$7.95	
	New Employee Orientation	46-7	$7.95	
	Professional Excellence for Secretaries	52-1	$7.95	
	Guide To Affirmative Action	54-8	$7.95	
	Writing A Human Resource Manual	70-X	$7.95	
	COMMUNICATIONS			
	Effective Presentation Skills	24-6	$7.95	
	Better Business Writing	25-4	$7.95	
	The Business of Listening	34-3	$7.95	
	Writing Fitness	35-1	$7.95	
	The Art of Communicating	45-9	$7.95	
	Technical Presentation Skills	55-6	$7.95	
	Making Humor Work For You	61-0	$7.95	
	Better Technical Writing	64-5	$7.95	
	Using Visual Aids in Business	77-7	$7.95	
	Influencing Others: A Practical Guide	84-X	$7.95	
	SELF-MANAGEMENT			
	Balancing Home And Career	10-6	$7.95	
	Mental Fitness: A Guide to Emotional Health	15-7	$7.95	
	Personal Financial Fitness	20-3	$7.95	
	Attitude: Your Most Priceless Possession	21-1	$7.95	
	Personal Time Management	22-X	$7.95	

(Continued on next page)

THE FIFTY-MINUTE SERIES

Quantity	Title	Code #	Price	Amount
	SELF-MANAGEMENT (CONTINUED)			
	Preventing Job Burnout	23-8	$7.95	
	Successful Self-Management	26-2	$7.95	
	Developing Positive Assertiveness	38-6	$7.95	
	Time Management And The Telephone	53-X	$7.95	
	Memory Skills In Business	56-4	$7.95	
	Developing Self-Esteem	66-1	$7.95	
	Creativity In Business	67-X	$7.95	
	Quality Awareness: A Personal Guide To Professional Standards	72-6	$7.95	
	Managing Personal Change	74-2	$7.95	
	Speedreading For Better Productivity	78-5	$7.95	
	Winning At Human Relations	86-6	$7.95	
	Stop Procrastinating	88-2	$7.95	
	SALES TRAINING/QUALITY CUSTOMER SERVICE			
	Sales Training Basics	02-5	$7.95	
	Restaurant Server's Guide	08-4	$7.95	
	Quality Customer Service	17-3	$7.95	
	Telephone Courtesy And Customer Service	18-1	$7.95	
	Professional Selling	42-4	$7.95	
	Customer Satisfaction	57-2	$7.95	
	Telemarketing Basics	60-2	$7.95	
	Calming Upset Customers	65-3	$7.95	
	Managing A Quality Service Organization	83-1	$7.95	
	ENTREPRENEURSHIP			
	Marketing Your Consulting Or Professional Services	40-8	$7.95	
	Starting Your Small Business	44-0	$7.95	
	Publicity Power	82-3	$7.95	
	CAREER GUIDANCE & STUDY SKILLS			
	Study Skills Strategies	05-X	$7.95	
	Career Discovery	07-6	$7.95	
	Plan B: Protecting Your Career From The Winds of Change	48-3	$7.95	
	I Got The Job!	59-9	$7.95	
	OTHER CRISP INC. BOOKS			
	Comfort Zones: A Practical Guide For Retirement Planning	00-9	$13.95	
	Stepping Up To Supervisor	11-8	$13.95	
	The Unfinished Business Of Living: Helping Aging Parents	19-X	$12.95	
	Managing Performance	23-7	$18.95	
	Be True To Your Future: A Guide to Life Planning	47-5	$13.95	
	Up Your Productivity	49-1	$10.95	
	How To Succeed In A Man's World	79-3	$7.95	
	Practical Time Management	275-4	$13.95	
	Copyediting: A Practical Guide	51-3	$18.95	

THE FIFTY-MINUTE SERIES
(Continued)

☐ Send volume discount information.

☐ Please send me a catalog.

	Amount
Total (from other side)	
Shipping ($1.50 first book, $.50 per title thereafter)	
California Residents add 7% tax	
Total	

Ship to: _____

_____

_____

_____

Phone number: _____

Bill to: _____

_____

_____

_____

P.O. # _____

All orders except those with a P.O.# must be prepaid.
For more information Call (415) 949-4888 or FAX (415) 949-1610.

BUSINESS REPLY

FIRST CLASS   PERMIT NO. 884   LOS ALTOS, CA

POSTAGE WILL BE PAID BY ADDRESSEE

Crisp Publications, Inc.
95 First Street
Los Altos, CA 94022

6467